PROJECTS FOR AUTUMN

Joan Jones

Illustrated by Stephen Wheele

Seasonal Projects
Projects for Spring
Projects for Summer
Projects for Autumn
Projects for Winter
Projects for Christmas
Projects for Easter

Seasons do not happen at the same time of year everywhere.
In the northern and southern halves of the world the seasons
are reversed, as this chart shows:

Northern Hemisphere			
Spring	*Summer*	*Autumn*	*Winter*
March	June	September	December
April	July	October	January
May	August	November	February
Autumn	*Winter*	*Spring*	*Summer*
Southern Hemisphere			

First published in 1989 by
Wayland (Publishers) Limited
61 Western Road, Hove
East Sussex BN3 1JD

Editor: Mike Hirst
Designer: Ross George

British Library Cataloguing in Publication Data
Jones, Joan
    Projects for autumn.
    1. Seasonal activities for children — For children
    I. Title II. Series
    790.1'922

ISBN 1-85210-368-X

© Copyright 1989 Wayland (Publishers) Ltd

Typeset by Direct Image Photosetting Limited, Hove, East Sussex
Printed and bound in Italy by Sagdos S.p.A., Milan

Contents

AUTUMN

The golden brown colours of an autumn landscape near Grasmere in northern England.

In each year there are four seasons; spring, summer, autumn and winter. Autumn is the third season of the year, between summer and winter. North of the Equator, in the northern hemisphere, September, October and November are generally regarded as the autumn months. In the southern hemisphere, in countries such as Australia and New Zealand, autumn occurs during the months of March, April and May.

Autumn is a time of change. Gradually the hours of daylight become fewer and the nights grow longer. The weather grows colder and there is often fog or mist. Particularly in the countryside, many things begin to look different. The flowers and colours of summer fade and some plants die. The leaves of many trees change colour from green to golden brown and eventually fall, so that twigs and branches are left bare.

Autumn is also the time when people must prepare for the winter months ahead. In many countries of the world, autumn is the time for the harvest. Farmers work long hours in the fields,

gathering the crops grown during the spring and summer. Many fruits and berries become ripe and ready to be picked.

Animals must prepare for the winter too. In autumn, some birds migrate and fly long distances to warmer countries where they will spend the winter. Other animals, such as hedgehogs and dormice, gather food and prepare for hibernation, their long winter sleep.

After the harvest, it is common for people to hold a religious celebration to give thanks for their crops. In the Christian Church, the harvest festival is one of the most important festivals of the year.

There are many other festivals in autumn too. In the United States, people remember the arrival of the early European settlers in their country at Thanksgiving. In October or early November, Hindus celebrate the important festival of Diwali, or the Festival of Lights.

013643

A FALLEN LEAF PICTURE

You will need:
- assorted leaves
- paper
- a pencil
- glue
- crayons or coloured pens

1 On your autumn walks gather a variety of autumn leaves.

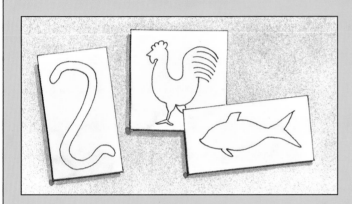

2 On a large piece of paper, draw the simple outline of an animal, perhaps a snake, a fish or a bird.

3 Lay the leaves on your picture, and overlap them to lie like feathers or scales.

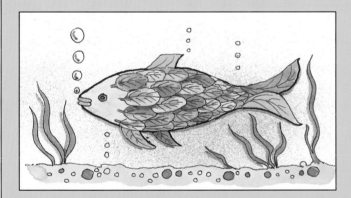

4 When you are happy with your arrangement, glue down the leaves. Add finishing touches like a beak or fins, and some grass, bubbles or waterweed.

5 When the glue has dried, cover your picture with a sheet of clean paper. Place some heavy books on top to press the picture flat.

THE CHANGING WEATHER

In the northern hemisphere, as winter approaches, the North Pole tilts away from the sun. This movement causes the days to grow cooler and the hours of daylight to decrease. Gradually the weather changes, bringing cold winds and rain, frost, mist and fog. In the southern hemisphere a similar change occurs when the South Pole begins to tilt away from the sun in March and April.

In early autumn, mists may rise over damp fields, rivers and canals. Moisture evaporates from the soil, and is also given off by leaves. If the air is warm, the moisture is absorbed into it and cannot be seen, but in the cooler days of autumn, such moisture hangs suspended as tiny droplets in the air. This moisture is mist. If it is very thick, it is called fog and can cause serious delays to land and air traffic.

In the early morning mists of autumn, spiders' webs show clearly in the hedges, hung with hundreds of dewdrops.

In some parts of the world frosts can occur early in the autumn. Frost is caused when the temperature falls to 0°C, the freezing point of water. Hoar frost can be particularly beautiful. It forms crystals, usually during the night, and appears in the morning like white whiskers on branches, fences, grass and plants.

Occasionally, in the northern hemisphere, a period of unusually warm weather will occur in autumn. It is called an Indian Summer. No one knows how it got its name but the American Indians knew of it and told early settlers in America that it would happen.

Dewdrops on a spider's web.

A SPIDER'S WEB

You will need:
- a piece of dark coloured card or paper
- grey or white paint and a thin paint brush, or a silver wax crayon
- mounting paper
- a few pipe cleaners
- glue
- a small bottle of fluorescent paint writer

1 Make a point somewhere near the centre of the paper.

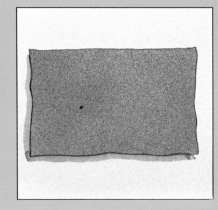

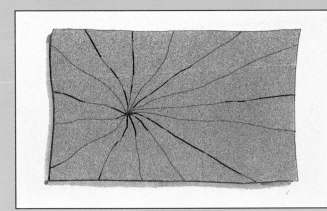

2 Using paint or wax crayon, draw a series of lines radiating from the centre to the edge of the paper.

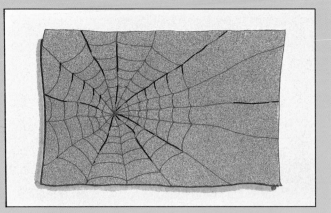

3 Working from the centre outwards, draw in the threads of the web.

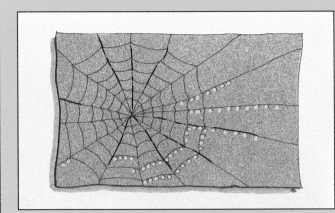

4 With the paint writer, drop tiny blobs of plastic paint on to the web. Make them hang down like dewdrops.

5 Make a little spider out of the pipe cleaners, and place it in the corner.

PLANTS AND TREES

In autumn, leaves lose their green colour and turn brown, red and yellow. Woods often look more beautiful in autumn than at any other time of year.

As the autumn days pass by, plants and grasses slowly fade and die. Their seeds have grown and blossomed, and now everything lies dormant again, waiting for another spring.

Some bushes are covered in berries, which will provide food for many birds and creatures through the winter months to come. Wasps and flies, in their search for food, pierce the skins of berries to reach the juice.

Plants now form seeds, from which new plants will grow in the coming year. The seeds of the ash tree change gradually from green to brown. They hang from the twigs in bunches, rattling in the wind. Shiny brown horse chestnuts form inside tough, spiky capsules. Acorns, the seeds of the oak tree, fall to the ground, ready to send down new roots in the following spring.

Plants spread their seeds in many different ways. Some form silky parachutes that carry seeds along on the wind. Others form pods that split and scatter their seeds around them. Many plants have seeds covered with tiny hooks that catch on clothes and animal fur. In this way, the seeds are carried away to grow in other places.

On pine trees, cones have formed and grown throughout the summer. On dry autumn days they open to let the ripe seeds inside scatter over the ground below.

WOODLAND WEIRDIES

You will need:

- **a selection of small, interesting twigs**
- **plaster**
- **small board**
- **glue**
- **oddments such as feathers, beads, lace, shells, etc.**

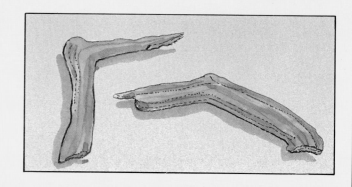

1 Study your twigs, letting them suggest to you the characters they could become.

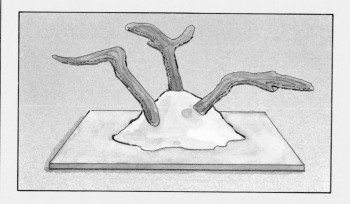

2 Mix up the plaster, place it on the board, and when it is nearly set, stand the twigs in it. They may need support until the plaster is dry.

3 Add feathers, beads, sequins and shells to your creature. Do not add too many pieces because they will clutter your creature and spoil it.

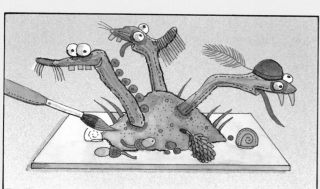

4 Paint the plaster base. When the paint is dry you could varnish it, and add finishing touches such as pebbles, snail shells, fir cones and acorns.

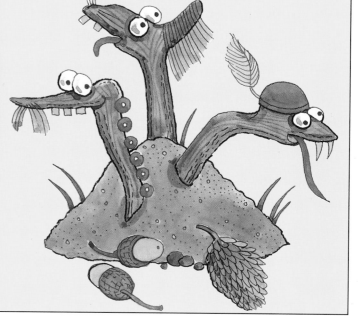

9

AUTUMN LEAVES

In autumn, the leaves of deciduous trees change colour. From their summer green they turn to yellow, red, russet and brown. They fall to the ground, twisting and turning through the air. It is fun to kick and scuff through the crisp dead leaves, and listen to the scrunching sound they make underfoot.

Growing leaves are full of moisture, which passes from them into the surrounding air. In the summer, this moisture is replaced by water from the soil. It is pumped up to the leaves from the tree's roots. In winter when the ground is cold and hard, the roots cannot absorb enough moisture to supply the leaves. This is the reason that trees must shed their leaves in autumn.

Where a leaf joins a twig, a layer of cork forms inside the joint. As winter approaches, the cork seals the veins that carry moisture to the leaves. The leaves die, and when frosts come and strong winds blow, they snap off and fall. The tree itself, however, is not dead. New buds have already formed and can be seen quite clearly. Small and tight, they are prepared to face the winter and will break into leaf as soon as spring comes again.

Autumn is a picturesque time of the year. In North America it is called the Fall. In Japan, the red leaves of the maple tree, and the yellow of the gingko add brilliant colour to the parks and gardens. During autumn, the Japanese love to go on walks and admire the beauty of their land.

MAKE A MAP OF AUTUMN

You will need:
- **a large sheet of paper**
- **colouring pencils or pens**

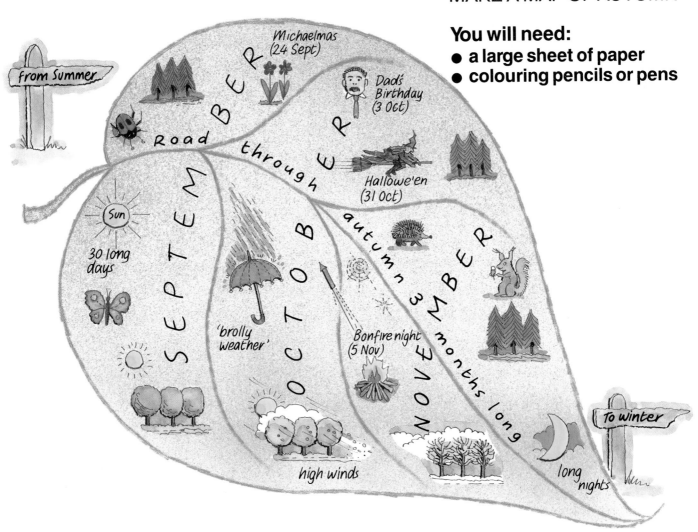

from Summer

Michaelmas (24 Sept)

Dad's Birthday (3 Oct)

Road through autumn 3 months long

SEPTEMBER

OCTOBER

NOVEMBER

Hallowe'en (31 Oct)

Sun

30 long days

'brolly weather'

Bonfire night (5 Nov)

high winds

long nights

To winter

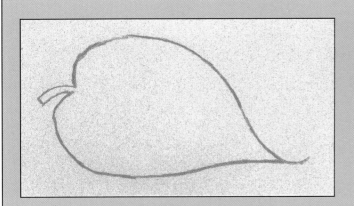

1 Draw an outline for your map in the shape of a leaf.

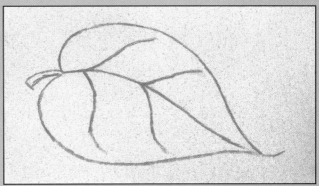

2 The central vein of the leaf can be the main road through autumn. The smaller veins can divide your map into different areas.

Dad's Birthday (3 Oct)

Michaelmas (24 Sept)

Hallowe'en (31 Oct)

3 On your map print some dates connected with the autumn months, and draw pictures next to them.

4 In each section of your leaf draw trees, first in leaf, then in autumn colours, and finally bare.

5 Add hedgehogs, butterflies, ladybirds and other animals.

Sun

30 long days

'brolly weather'

long nights

6 Show the changing weather.

HARVEST TIME

In many countries of the world, autumn is the time of the harvest. Farmers work long hours in the fields to gather in produce which has grown and ripened during the summer. After the harvest, the produce is sold or stored away to last the winter months.

In North America, there are huge stretches of farmland, called the prairies, where cereals are harvested in the autumn. The Canadian prairies produce large amounts of wheat. In the United States, there is a huge plain called the corn belt. Maize is the main crop on the corn belt and in some places it grows taller than a fully-grown person. It grows quickly too, sometimes as much as 5 cm in a single night.

In the southern United States another important crop is the cotton plant from which cloth is made. It grows well throughout the long, warm summer, and the dry autumn weather is ideal for picking the raw cotton.

In India, Japan, and other countries in the Far East, the rice crop is gathered in the autumn, and fresh seed sown for the following spring. Australia grows wheat, oats, barley and sugar, all of which must be harvested in the autumn months. In California,

This couple is harvesting rice, one of the main crops in Japan.

and countries around the Mediterranean, ripened grapes are picked and made into wine.

Today, most grapes are picked by machine, which is quicker than gathering by hand. Care must be taken to pick the grapes at just the right time or the wine will be spoiled. The grapes are transported to factories where they are crushed and mixed with yeast and sugar to make wine. In the past, grapes were crushed by foot, but today they are crushed by huge rollers.

AN ELDERBERRY DRINK FOR AUTUMN

You will need:
- one or two bottles with tops
- ½ large saucepan of ripe fresh elderberries
- 500 grammes of sugar for every ½ litre of liquid
- 1 teaspoon ginger
- 1 teaspoon cinnamon
- 12 cloves

Safety note:
Be careful when boiling the elderberries. Ask an adult to help you.

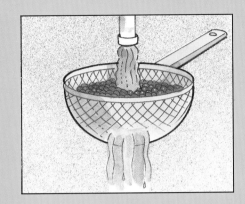

1 Wash the berries and put them in a large saucepan. Cover with cold water, but do not have the saucepan more than half full.

2 Bring to the boil and simmer for half an hour until the juice is out of the berries. Leave to cool.

3 Press the berries through a sieve. Collect the juice in a pan and measure it.

4 Add the remaining ingredients. Add 500 grammes of sugar to every ½ litre of liquid.

5 Bring the mixture to the boil, and then simmer for half an hour, stirring often.

6 When the mixture has cooled, pour it into bottles using a funnel.
   One tablespoon of elderberry drink in a mug of hot water is very soothing when you have a cold.

HARVEST FESTIVALS

Gathering in the crops is an important event in all farming communities. People are thankful and happy if the harvest is plentiful. From earliest times, harvest has been a period of joy, with celebration and merry-making for people living in countries throughout the world.

In Britain, harvest festivals were once held in barns and fields, but in the nineteenth century a special church Thanksgiving Service was started. It quickly became very popular, and was soon accepted as an important part of the Christian calendar.

Harvest festival is still celebrated today. Churches are decorated with sheaves of corn, fruit, vegetables and flowers. Special loaves of bread are baked for the service. Some are made to look like sheaves of corn.

Today, many schools hold their own harvest festivals, and still follow the old church tradition of distributing the produce afterwards to hospitals and local charities.

Some of the earliest settlers in Australia and New Zealand were British. Today, farmers in these countries celebrate harvest festival in much the same way as in Britain. However, because autumn in the southern hemisphere falls between March and May, they hold it at a different time of year.

In Japan, people give thanks for the rice harvest at an important festival called the New Taste Festival. This is held on 23 November and is a national holiday. Thanksgiving festivals for a good harvest are held in Africa too, and in some Arab countries, prayers are said to Allah, asking for a good crop again the following year.

Making a harvest basket.

MAKE A HARVEST BASKET

You will need:
- **a small cardboard box**
- **tissue paper**
- **ribbon**
- **a sheet of brightly coloured wrapping paper**
- **Clingfilm**
- **glue**
- **fruit and vegetables**

1 Place the cardboard box on the inside of the wrapping paper.

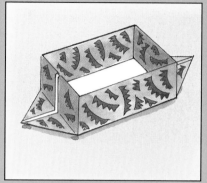

2 Fold the paper neatly over the long edges of the box.

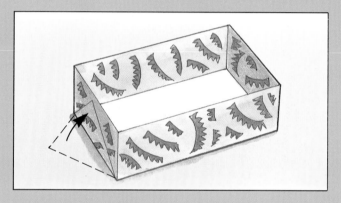

3 Crease the flap carefully and glue it to the side of the box.

4 Cover the bottom of the box with tissue paper, tucking in the edges.

5 Fill the box with fruit and vegetables, arranging them attractively.

6 Cover with Clingfilm and add a bow of ribbon.

PREPARING FOR WINTER

During the spring and summer months a farmer feeds his sheep and cows on as much fresh grass as possible. In the winter, when the snow falls and the ground is frozen hard, grass does not grow, and livestock find it hard to survive in the bitter cold. Some farmers grow catch crops in the first weeks of autumn. In fields where the harvest has been gathered early, grass and rye are sown, and if the weather is warm, the crop will grow quickly and provide extra food for the animals.

Autumn is one of the busiest times of the year for farmers in New Zealand. During the summer, the sheep roam free over wild and steep mountains. When autumn comes it is time to move them on to lower pastures, where the weather will be warmer during the winter months. The gathering up of sheep from the mountains is called the big muster, and is the work of many people and sheepdogs.

In parts of Austria too, the cows are brought from the high pasture in the autumn. They are led from the higher ground through the villages. Their cowbells tinkle as they walk and their heads and

The big muster in New Zealand. Farmers must bring thousands of sheep down from the hills before winter weather sets in.

necks are adorned with flowers, ribbon and tinsel. Sometimes a girl leads the procession, distributing pastries to the onlookers as she goes.

In some parts of Yugoslavia, Italy and Portugal, people still collect firewood in autumn in the traditional way. Wood is carried down the hillsides by donkeys and is stacked outside sheds and houses ready for the winter.

MAKE A PAPIER–MACHE COWBELL

You will need:
- a lump of Plasticine the size of a tennis ball
- Vaseline
- strips of torn newspaper about 2.5 cm wide
- strips of torn white tissue paper about 2.5 cm wide
- a jam jar of cold water paste
- scissors
- paint or coloured pens
- ribbon
- a small bell

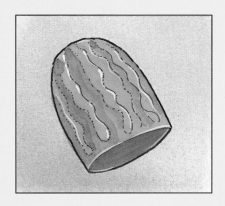

1 Model a cowbell with the Plasticine. Cover it with Vaseline.

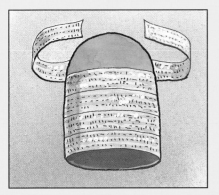

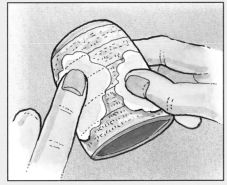

2 Paste a few strips of newspaper and wrap them around the Plasticine, overlapping each strip.

3 Continue to cover the Plasticine until there are six or seven layers of papier mâché. Use plenty of paste and smooth it down well with your fingers.

4 Cover the newspaper with tissue paper until the newsprint no longer shows through. Leave the cowbell to dry for about a week.

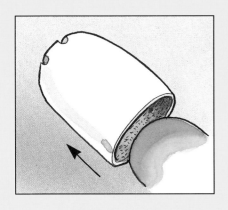

5 When the papier mâché is dry, remove the Plasticine. Trim the mouth of the bell.

6 Decorate the bell. Thread a ribbon, with bell attached, through two holes in the top to make a handle.

MIGRATION

When autumn arrives, some birds grow restless. They know that winter is approaching and that food will be scarce if they stay where they are. Instinct tells them that they must fly to a warmer country where food will be more plentiful. The journeys that birds make can cover many hundreds of kilometres and are part of the process called migration.

Many migrating birds are insect eaters. They include swallows, cuckoos, swifts, martins and warblers. Swallows breed in many parts of the northern hemisphere, but when autumn arrives they move south to find a winter home. They travel to places as far away as Africa, Argentina and even Australia.

Other migrants include ducks and wading birds. These birds fly south from the Arctic regions where lakes and marshes freeze over during the long northern winter. Sea birds like the auk leave their breeding grounds to spend the winter on the open sea, and in the southern hemisphere, some penguins move to warmer areas before winter begins.

Even some species of butterfly migrate. One of the best known is the American monarch or milkweed. It spreads into Canada for the summer, but in early autumn it gathers in huge swarms and moves south into Mexico and Florida.

No one really knows how migrating creatures find their way. They know by instinct when and where to go. Even young birds, abandoned by their parents, manage to make long journeys on their own.

Canada geese outlined against the autumn sky as they fly south for the winter.

A BUTTERFLY ON BALSA WOOD

You will need:
- **a piece of thin balsa wood approximately 18 cm by 12 cm**
- **coloured pens**
- **a picture of a butterfly**
- **mounting card**

1 With a pale coloured pen, copy the outline of a butterfly on to the balsa wood.

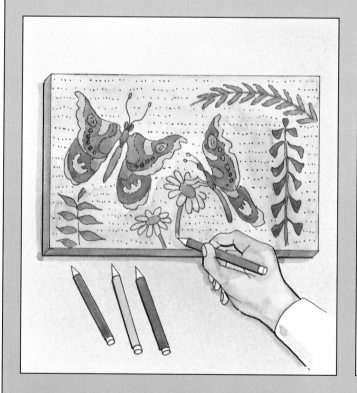

2 Colour the butterfly. Make it bright and add some flowers and a few leaves to the picture.

3 Mount your picture and put a border round it.

CHIMNEYS

Hampton Court Palace in London was built about five hundred years ago. Can you see the ornamental designs around the tall chimneys?

After the warm days of summer, the cooler autumn weather warns people that winter is approaching and that they will soon have to begin heating their homes. Today, many people have gas and electric heating, but in the past, open fires were more usual. Every house had a hearth, or fireplace, for heating. Fires were made using wood, coal or turf for fuel. Smoke made by the open fires was taken out of the house by the chimney, and up until quite recently, all houses were built with chimneys. Today however, not all buildings have chimneys, and if you look at the roofs of some modern houses, you will not be able to see any chimney pots.

Although some chimney pots are very plain and simple, houses built by rich people often had elaborate, ornamental chimneys. The pots can be round, square, oval or even octagonal shaped, and are different all over the world. In Elizabethan England, chimneys were part of a house's decoration and some chimneys even had flower and leaf designs carved on them.

A chimney which is in use must be cleaned regularly to remove the dust and grime which collects inside. In the past, chimney sweeps were a common sight, going from house to house with sets of long, extendible brushes. Traditionally, they were believed to bring good fortune, and although few people today need to have their chimney cleaned by a sweep, it is still thought to be lucky if a sweep comes to a wedding.

A MINIATURE CHIMNEY–POT PLANT HOLDER

You will need:
- **cold clay**
- **a small jar or plastic cylinder**
- **a jar of water**
- **paints**
- **clear varnish**

1 Place the cylinder upside down on a small board. Rub the cold clay in your hand until it is soft and workable.

2 Mould the clay around the outside of the container until the sides are about ½ cm thick. Use water to help in modelling the clay.

3 Score lines on the cold clay to make it look like blocks of stone. Cover the top of the container with a layer of clay.

4 Turn chimney upside down. Add some decoration to the top of the chimney, and leave it for several days to dry.

5 When it is completely dry, paint the clay to make it look like old stone. You can also varnish it to give it a sheen.

6 You can fill the container with compost and grow a small plant in it.

HIBERNATION

Winter can be a difficult time of year for many animals. There is little to eat, and the weather can be very cold. Some creatures hide away and enter a deep sleep called hibernation. Their body temperature can fall to freezing point, and they seem to be dead. They hardly breathe, and their heartbeat is very faint.

Among the animals which hibernate are bats, hamsters, dormice and hedgehogs. Snails and ladybirds hide away and sleep throughout the winter too, but they do not truly hibernate.

During the autumn, hibernating creatures must prepare for their long sleep. Some gather and store food in case they should wake and feel hungry. Some grow thicker coats or put on weight. This weight forms as fat which will nourish the body during the coming months.

This hedgehog has curled itself up tightly into a ball before going into hibernation.

Some species of bat search for cellars, caves or hollow trees. Others prefer dark, uninhabited buildings where they can sleep dry and undisturbed until the spring.

The dormouse hibernates underground or in a hollow tree. It tucks in its head, curls up small and wraps its furry tail tightly around its body. Hedgehogs build nests of dead leaves. These nests are so comfortable and snug that bees and mice have been known to take them over when the hedgehog leaves at the end of winter. Hedgehogs may prepare several nests in different places but, having found their favourite, they rarely move unless it is destroyed.

KNIT A LADYBIRD

You will need:

- one ball bright red wool
- average sized knitting needles
- seven black felt circles about 1.5 cm across
- 3 black or red pipe cleaners
- some old rags cut into small pieces for stuffing
- a big-eyed sewing needle
- fabric glue

1 Knit a rectangle about 30 cm by 9 cm in red wool.

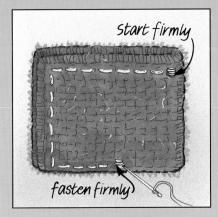

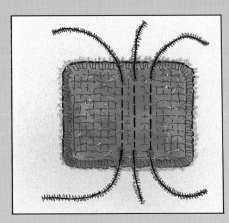

2 Fold the rectangle in half and stitch it up along two and a half sides. Turn it inside out.

3 Push the pipe cleaners through on the underside to form legs. Bend to make leg joints.

4 Fill the inside of the ladybird with stuffing and stitch up the open edge.

5 Glue felt circles on to the ladybird. Stitch its body lines in black wool.

6 Add eyes and a mouth to your ladybird.

MARTINMAS

Saint Martin of Tours was a popular saint in France and England during the Middle Ages. He was born in Hungary, but was educated in Italy, where he first heard about Christianity.

When his education was finished, he was sent into military service. According to legend, one day he met a beggar who was starving and dying of cold. Martin was so concerned that he tore his own cloak in two and gave one half to the beggar. Later, in a dream, the beggar revealed himself as Christ and told the angels of Saint Martin's good deed.

Martin became a priest, then a bishop, and eventually was made Pope. However, he made enemies because he would not let the government interfere in church affairs. He was banished to the Crimea, where he died because nobody cared for him. Years later, Martin was recognized as a great martyr and was made a saint. A special feast day, called Martinmas, is held for him each year. It falls on 11 November.

In the Middle Ages, Martinmas was a busy day. It was the day on which animals had to be killed because there was not enough food to keep them through the winter. Their meat was then dried and salted to stop it going bad.

When Martin became Bishop of Tours he was said to have hidden himself away, but cackling geese betrayed his hiding place. As a result, it became the custom for people to eat goose on Saint Martin's Day.

Saint Martin, tearing his cloak in half to give to the beggar. This illustration comes from a handwritten book, made in France almost six hundred years ago.

A MODEL OF ST. MARTIN

In parts of Italy, people make clay models of St. Martin and the beggar to whom he gave his cloak.

You will need:
- modelling dough
- clear varnish
- a modelling board

For the dough:
- one mug plain flour
- ⅓ mug cooking salt
- cold water to mix

You will need an adult to help you with the baking.

1 Mix together the flour and salt. Add enough water to make a smooth dough. It should not stick to your hands.

2 Place the dough on a floured board, and flatten it out to about ½ cm thick.

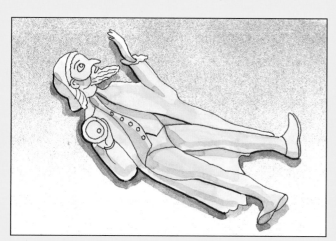

3 Model Saint Martin or the beggar. Put in plenty of detail such as eyes, mouth, ears, fingers, and a beard. A small manicure stick is useful for modelling fine detail.

4 Lay your model on a greased baking tray, and bake in a hot oven until it is firm but not brown. Paint and varnish the model when it has cooled.

DIWALI

A huge dummy of Ravana, the wicked demon with ten heads. At the end of the Ramlila performance this dummy will be set on fire, to celebrate Prince Ram's victory.

Diwali is one of the most important festivals in the Hindu calendar. It takes place in October or November, on the darkest night of late autumn.

At Diwali, Hindus remember the mythological life story of King Ram, who is one of the best-loved Hindu gods. While still a young prince, Ram was banished from his kingdom by the wicked queen. For many years, Ram lived in the forest with his wife, Sita and his brother Lakshman. Then one day, whilst Ram was out hunting, Sita was kidnapped by Ravana, a demon with ten heads.

Ram and Lakshman followed Ravana to his castle and, helped by Hanuman the monkey god, killed Ravana and rescued Sita. They then returned to Ram's kingdom, at Ayodhya, where Ram was joyfully welcomed by the people as king.

Many Hindus believe that the Ram story sets them an example of how to behave. They try themselves to be as good and brave as Ram and Sita.

In the month before Diwali, people in towns and cities throughout north India perform a play which tells the Ram story. It is called the Ramlila. Often at the end of the play a huge effigy, or dummy, of Ravana is burnt. There are even children's comic books which tell the Ram story too.

At Diwali itself, everyone decorates their house. Tiny oil lamps are placed outside doors, on window ledges and on balconies. These lamps give light to show Ram the way home to Ayodhya. There are lots of fireworks and families get together for parties. It is also the custom to give presents and boxes of sweets, such as *barfi*, to friends and relations.

MAKING BARFI

You will need:
- **3 cups full fat milk powder**
- **2 tablespoons double cream**
- **1 cup sugar**
- **¾ cup water**

Optional flavours:
- **¼ teaspoon nutmeg**
- **2 teaspoons crushed almonds**
- **2 teaspoons pistachios**
- **¼ teaspoon crushed cardamom**

1 Mix the double cream and milk powder until it becomes crumbly.

2 Heat the water slowly and stir in the sugar to make a syrup. After about 15 minutes, bring to the boil.

3 Cool the syrup slightly and add the remaining ingredients.

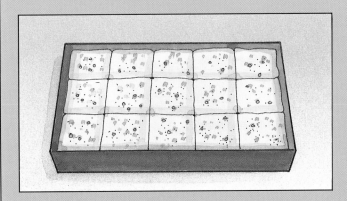

4 Spread the mixture in a rectangular tray covered in Clingfilm. Leave to cool before slicing into pieces.

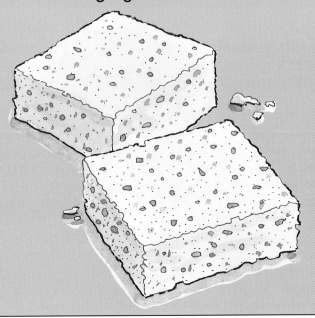

THANKSGIVING DAY

In the autumn of 1620, a group of people set sail from England, in a ship called the *Mayflower*. They were bound for America, only recently discovered by Europeans. They had been persecuted in England because of their religious beliefs, and they hoped to live peacefully in the New World.

After a difficult journey, they landed in what is now the United States. It was December and too late to sow the seeds they had taken with them. The winter was severe, and over half of the company died. Without the help of friendly local people, everyone might have perished.

Those people who were left worked throughout the following spring and summer. Their crops grew, and the harvest was so successful that it was decided to hold a festival of thanksgiving where local people and settlers celebrated together.

A Thanksgiving display of pumpkins and ornamental corn. Particularly in Canada, pumpkin pie forms an important part of the Thanksgiving dinner.

Today, Thanksgiving Day is a popular national festival in the United States and Canada. Families come together to give thanks for peace and plenty. Many attend church in the morning, and there are sporting events later in the day. Dinner is a family time when roast turkey, stuffing and cranberry sauce are served with white and sweet potatoes, followed by apple or pumpkin pie.

Over the years, the date of Thanksgiving Day has been changed many times. Today it is celebrated on the last Thursday of November in the United States, and the second Monday of October in Canada.

A FAMILY TREE

You will need:

- **a small spray of twigs**
- **pale coloured thin card**
- **crayons or coloured pens**
- **plaster**
- **a brush**
- **a small board about 12 cm square**
- **coloured thread or ribbon**

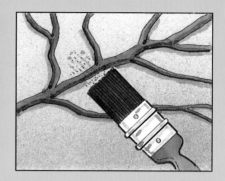

1 Brush down your spray of twigs to remove any dirt, dust or moss.

2 Mix the plaster and place it in a mound on the board. When it has nearly set, stick the twigs in it.

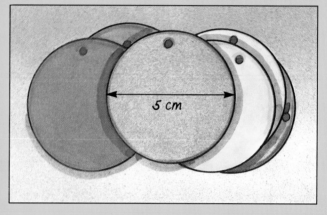

3 Cut out a circle of card, 5 cm across, for each member of your family. Make a hole for the ribbon or thread.

Martin Simon
born
10 July 1978

4 On one side of the card draw a picture of one member of your family. On the other side print her or his name, and their date of birth.

5 Add the ribbon or thread to the card and hang it on to one of your twigs.

Glossary

Absorb To soak up or drink in liquid.

Catch crop An extra crop grown quickly, usually in autumn, after the main crop has been harvested.

Deciduous Deciduous trees lose their leaves every autumn.

Dormant Asleep.

Evaporate To dry up.

Extendible Something which can be extended or made longer.

Hemisphere Half of the Earth.

Hibernation To hide away and sleep through the winter.

Martyr A person who gives up his or her life for their beliefs.

Migrate To move from one place to another, usually over a long distance.

Mythological Concerning a myth, or ancient story about gods or heroes.

Octagonal Eight-sided.

Persecute To harm or punish someone because of their beliefs.

Russet A reddish brown colour.

Books to read

Michael Cooper   *Weather*   (Granada, 1983)
Esmond Harris   *Trees*
   (Piccolo: A Piper Book, 1986)
Sukhbir Singh Kapoor   *Sikh Festivals*
   (Wayland, 1985)
Swasti Mitter   *Hindu Festivals*   (Wayland, 1985)
Malcolm Penny   *Animal Migration*
   (Wayland, 1987)
John Pohlman   *All about the Weather*
   (Hamlyn, 1984)
Ingrid Selberg   *Trees and Leaves*
   (Usborne, 1977)
John Snelling   *Buddhist Festivals*
   (Wayland, 1985)
Ralph Whitlock   *Harvest and Thanksgiving*
   (Wayland, 1984)

Picture acknowledgements

Barnaby's Picture Library 6, 8, 16; Bridgeman Art Library 24; Cephas Picture Library 20; Oxford Scientific Films 4, 18, 22; Bury Peerless 26; Wayland Picture Library 12; Timothy Woodcock cover, 14.

Cover artwork is by John Yates.

Index